UNLOCKING THE SECRETS OF NETWORKING

By: Alicia Veillon

Table of Contents

Introduction

When I was younger, we lived in a very small town where everybody knew everybody. In our little town, I lived right across the street from the courthouse. Every morning while I was getting ready for school, my father would disappear to have coffee with all the fellas over at the courthouse. My father, who is an electrician and a contractor, would spend hours there. When I would ask somebody, "What is Dad doing over there all the time?" They would laugh and say, "He's a politikin'" I had no idea what that meant since I knew he had no intentions of running for office. Later in life, I would find out that his "politikin' meant that he was keeping his ear to the ground, so to speak. He was listening to the vibrations of the town to know where to find the best jobs and the best connections to those jobs. Understanding the ebb and flow of the local economy is both an art and a science, and my dad's trips to the courthouse allowed him to experience the beauty of relationship building. This is when I discovered the true genius of networking.

After intently studying my dad's behavior, I started to become intrigued with networking as a whole. This may be when my passion was born. As an entrepreneur, the aspect I enjoy and excel at the most is networking. I've spent years expanding my network, and I have discovered that effective networking has the potential to connect you with someone that may change your life. Relationships are becoming the most essential component of a business and can determine its overall success or failure.

It doesn't matter if you are a small business owner, a CEO of a large corporation, or an employee, this book is for you. Relationships are the foundation for everything that we do, especially in business. There is so much to learn, when it comes to this subject. Even if you have a phone filled with contacts, you should always try to learn how to effectively connect to others. The information that you are about to receive will help you find new contacts, new partners to work with, and new customers because nowadays this has become a huge factor in where your business is going. A person doesn't need to attend hundreds of events and collect a million business cards to be successful, but getting out there and networking with an actual plan will definitely result in more meaningful business relationships that are imperative to the future of any healthy company.

Successful entrepreneurs always need to be seeking opportunities to connect so they can grow their sphere of influence. What is a sphere of influence? It's who you know not what you know. It does not matter who you are or what you do; every person has a sphere of influence. Your sphere of influence starts with your family and friends and expands to your chosen career field.

So, now I want you to ask yourself, "Who do I know, like, and trust?" The answer to this question will give you direction for where to start building your sphere. Once you determine that, you must determine how you will build your sphere. Networking is one of the best and quickest ways to build it.

You may have negative emotions attached to networking. Have you ever felt this way after you hear the word 'networking'?

- It doesn't work for me

- It cost too much

- I never have enough time

- I'm too busy

- I never meet the right people

- Everyone is too salesy

- I feel pushed

I can provide an endless list of reasons why people feel that networking is not a good fit for them or their business. You may be apprehensive about it, but I want you to think about this. What could you be missing? Do you have a storefront business that has numerous customers visiting every day? Are you a service-type business whose schedule is filled from dawn to dusk? Will your friends and family be able to support you with a significant income that you can retire from?

Could the community and general public benefit from knowing about what you do? Could your business afford to grow even more?

Let's look at 'why' you do what you do. What is your true why? What motivates you to get out of bed every morning? What drives you to work at such a high level everyday? Is your business connected to your passion?

Sometimes, I network because I can't contain my passion. For me, my passion is directly connected to my business. Why would I just keep it to myself? I feel like the world needs to know how I can help them. So, to me networking has become the most valuable asset in my business, and every single contact that I make becomes a part of my growing inventory. Therefore, I actually 'make' time to network.

It's a part of my calendar of activities, and it's a part of my marketing plan for the year. I enjoy learning about other industries as well. It's one of the ways I enjoy staying competitive in my own industry. Networking helps a business in many ways. It allows you to gain more speaking points and become aware of hot topics happening in your industry. Also, networking really helps you to become a connector, which is an invaluable asset.

Never forget, learning how to network effectively is one of the most crucial skills any entrepreneur can attain. How else will you meet contacts and future clients that are necessary to grow your business? It's important to realize that people want to buy products or services from people they know, like, and trust. People invest in people before they invest in anything material. Nobody uses the phone book anymore to look up businesses. They use phone books to prop open doors, recycle and kindle fires. When someone is looking for their next hairdresser, someone to do their nails, a plumber, or a travel agent, most of the time they're going to ask a friend if they know, like, and trust a business that provides their desired services.

Word-of-mouth referrals have become much more common in today's market. It's similar to the good old boy network of the past that operated on phrases such as, "You pat my back and I'll pat yours," so to speak. The current problem is that many business owners have lost the talent for making connections.

Just so that you know, business owners and sales people can and do succeed without ever networking. But,

I can tell you that without networking, they are working 10 times harder to generate business than those in the same industry that practice and participate in networking. Networking will put you in touch with people that you otherwise never would have reached. At its core, networking is a relationship-building machine.

What is Networking?

The Small Business Encyclopedia defines networking as, "Developing and using contacts made in business for purposes beyond the reason for the initial contact." In other words, the purpose of networking is to meet and then form relationships with other people that you will continue to build after the initial meeting. I have been to so many networking events in my career that just didn't accomplish this goal.

In the beginning, I felt like I was wasting my time and money. But, I believed in networking because if I could obtain the skill of meeting other entrepreneurs and cultivate the right relationships, then I was certain that it would be a major win for my business. I knew what I needed to do. I needed to take it to a higher skill set and learn how to master networking like no other.

In my journey towards mastery, I discovered that networking was more than just getting out and meeting people. I also discovered it was more than just collecting business cards. I have thousands of cards, but that in no way signifies networking success. I had to decide where to even to begin.

What did I need to learn?

Who did I need to contact?

How much was it going to cost me?

And how do I make this an effective part of growing a business?

Overall, when considering a marketing budget, networking really is an effective low-cost way to advertise your business while branding yourself and your company to your local community. But before we get started, I want to remind you that it's called, net-"work". Like anything that is valuable in your business, it will take work.

Which Networking Event Is Right For Me And My Business?

Here is a particular subject that is definitely well worth reviewing because I have been to several networking events that really weren't a good fit for me or my business. Here are four things you must do before attending an event.

1. Do your research ahead of time.

2. Look at the previous events by the same host or the organization's type to see what they have to offer.

3. Check and see if the sponsors or maybe the guest list is available. Sometimes it helps to see if you share common connections with different guests.

4. Request an introduction ahead of time, and if there's a company in the house that you might have a particular interest in, find resources that provide information on who they are.

The beautiful thing is that you will have many events to choose from. There are so many different events that you can participate in or even become a member. So, let's talk about what you should be looking for so that you can decide what's a good fit for you.

There are different categories of networking called lead groups, referral groups, virtual online groups, and professional associations. You can even become a part of your local organizations like the Chamber of Commerce. Even with all those distinctions, there are still other areas that you need to look at when considering events such as size, requirements, goals, cost, time, frequency, and other attendees. You also need to take into account what kind of business are you representing. That could be a big factor into what type of group works best for your business.

Where to Find Networking Events?

When I first moved into my area, I did not know one single soul, but I had a business to run and clientele to service. I knew I needed more client acquisition, so I started asking myself vital questions. Where do I find people? New clients? New customers? New partnerships? I will give you some of the answers to these questions, and the process I used to help me gain more clients and significantly increase my impact.

First, I determined what type of network I wanted to associate with, as there are several different types such as:

Community service clubs

These can be a lot of fun since there is the potential to form many long-term relationships in organizations like the Rotary Club, Lions Club, and Kiwanis.

Membership Organizations

There are some network groups that meet weekly for the purpose of exchanging referrals. These usually restrict membership by profession or specialty and have very stringent meeting formats. They have an application, screening process, and membership dues. Most of them meet weekly or bi-weekly and have a high code of ethics and quality standards. Organizations like BNI, Le Tip, and

Biz to Biz require a commitment, which you typically pay in time and dues. Then there are those that are modified versions of this which include, Radical Referrals, Pink Polka Dot, 4br and hundreds of others.

All-Inclusive Organizations

These are networking groups that offer an open membership to anyone regardless of the profession. Typically, these are organizations like the Chamber of Commerce and different groups that include many entrepreneurs within the community. Again, these organizations and groups are designed to help develop word-of-mouth based referrals because they allow you to meet many other business men and women.

Women's Only Groups

There is a growing number of these types of networking groups. They are very diverse and come in many types. These would be great for businesses that are women-owned or businesses that target female customers.

Social Organizations

Some organizations create opportunities for you to meet other people, but they also include an element of fun. Organizations such as Jaycees, is an environment that offers fun along with networking opportunities.

Professional Organizations

These organizations are usually connected with your profession. For example, the American Bar Association, Teachers Association, and Lawyers Association are groups that are comprised of people from similar industries. There are so many types out there depending upon your career field.

Online Organizations

One of the most successful places I have used to find networking groups in my area was meetup.com. This site offers many meetup groups that you can search based on your interests, age group, gender, or overall networking goal. There is also LinkedIn.com. This site is typically associated with specific industries, but it often posts events that interested people can attend.

Eventbrite.com is another site that offers networking opportunities through specific events. The site easily categorizes a search of local upcoming events. They have anything from casual social mixers to formal panel discussions.

Of course, you can always ask local business owners to give shout outs on Facebook, and it won't be long before you'll be so well-connected that you'll have your choice of networking events to attend.

Three great questions to ask yourself are, "Where do my customers go to network?" "What business organizations would benefit my business?" and "How can I build my image or my business's image in the community?" I never restrict myself to just one type of networking, as I never like to limit my potential.

After you attend a networking event, always ask yourself it gave you great value? Be aware that there are some people that just want to trade dollar for dollar in a social atmosphere, and they call it business networking. The problem with this is that no one ever truly grows a business by simply the "you buy from me, I buy from you" approach.

Things to Know, Before You Go!

I can't tell you how many times we as business owners have been in shock at the things we have seen at local networking events. From the expectations of the attendees to people's attitudes, there can be many unexpected occurrences that happen at these events.

Present Your Best Self

Seriously, networking events are not places you go to looking like you just crawled out of the bed from in between the mattresses, or you just recovered from the flu. These events are opportunities for you to look your best. You are representing your brand and your business, so clean clothes and a shower are a must. Good grooming goes such a long way because first impressions really do matter. Even if you work as an employee of your company, when you go out to a networking event and you are the representing the owner of your company, you may have to go home, get a shower, and put on the appropriate attire.

So, fellow entrepreneurs, it's time to "suit up" for your business and come in your uniform. Be prepared to represent your business with class and professionalism.

You also need to have posture. What is posture? Posture is simply confidence in knowing who you are and why you are there.

Positive Attitude

Be friendly and approachable with a smile. Bring some energy with you. Introduce yourself to others, and start up the conversation. Make business suggestions to other attendees or even give them a referral. Not only will you make a friend, but helping others will eliminate your own self-consciousness. It's a great side benefit. Oh, and remember what goes around comes around. If you make an obvious effort to help others, you'll soon find others helping you as well.

Body Language

I can understand that there will be times that you are having a "bad" day. Sometimes you will have to put on an act or a performance because you're at the event to do a job. You're on the clock, so to speak. The last thing you may feel like doing is being there, but at that point, it doesn't matter. You are already there, which means you should make the best of it and purpose in your mind to have a successful event.

Your body language is very important. Be aware of how you stand, where you place your hands, and the look on your face. If you're standing over in a corner with your arms crossed, you're probably not going to get many connections. This will make you seem unapproachable, closed off, and unwelcoming.

If you are not smiling, but reflecting on something that upset you earlier in the day, it will show on your face. If you are eating alone at the corner table, you will seem isolative. Look around, check out the body language of others. It does make a difference in how others perceive you.

Be Prepared

Do you have your business cards with you and do you have enough of them? Make sure they are very clear with a large enough font with an appeasing color combination. I can't tell you how many black business cards with small red cursive print I've received and had to throw away. I've also received business cards without the phone number or an email. You need to have all your relevant information on your business card.

What if you run out? Or you are a new business owner? Don't fret! Make up little flyers to hand out. Just have enough on hand so that you can exchange contact information with the connections you make at the event.

Practice your elevator speech

An elevator speech is simply a few sentences that summarizes you and your business in a positive light. This is an opportunity to create interest. Your goal should be to forge a connection and create curiosity about you and what you do. It might serve you well to have several versions of your elevator speech on hand. Work hard to customize it to your intended audience. Be able to pivot and change directions as needed.

You are also going to want to practice looking "through the person" you're talking to. In other words, don't just focus on the person in front of you, focus on the 250 contacts they have in their sphere of influence. The reason for this is that the person you are talking to may or may not need your products or service, but they will know others who do.

Tools for Networking

When you go to a networking event, you are on the job, so yes, you will need your toolbox. The first thing you're going to need is a smile. Next you're going to need a great attitude. A positive, uplifting attitude attracts that same positive energy. You may have to sit out in the car and listen to some blood pumping music to make this happen, but before you go into that room with these people, make sure that your energy stays positive. Once you enter the room, you are in performance mode. Leave everything else in the car. Leave the issues and concerns that are happening at home, with the family, at the job, or anything else that can disrupt your pattern of amazingness.

You also need to make sure that you have your current information on business cards or fliers. You must decide which form is the best way to present your information? Also, does your information stand out from everybody else?

It has already been mentioned but deserves further attention. Look at your cards or fliers and determine if they have an appealing font, color and enough information? Is the information that you included create intrigue? Does it create a desire for them to want to get to know you and your business more?

I want to cover something very important here. Whatever you do, don't just go to the event and throw these in the air like 52 card pick-up. Don't leave them in the bathroom, on the tables, or on the chairs at the bar. This is extremely poor taste. Cards should be exchanged during meaningful conversations, so that they can be a resource for further connection.

During the Event

You're here, you're dressed to impress, and you're ready for action. Hopefully, you are early or at least on time. This is a key indicator of how you run your business. It also shows how you run your meetings and treat your associates. Your punctuality shows others whether or not you can be trusted with their clients, family and friends on an appointment. Punctuality definitely sends a message!

Now, how do you extract the most value from this event that you have chosen?

When you arrive at the event, there are some strategies that you can use to make your event more successful depending upon your goal for the night. Check your attitude, your uniform, your smile, your posture and be ready to work the room.

Place your name tag on your left side so when you shake hands people can see it better. Repeat to yourself, "This is about givers' gain." Recheck your attitude while you are working the room. Remember to be interested, not interesting.

Look for the people standing alone. Approach them, introduce yourself ,and help them feel comfortable.

Whether you believe it or not, a lot of people are experiencing the same exact feelings of nervousness and fear you may be feeling. Being relaxed, or letting people think that you are, will be contagious to others as well and make them feel more comfortable when talking to you.

By the way, how is your handshake? This is a huge indicator of your level of confidence. No one likes a limp handshake, and at the same time, no one likes it to be so firm their knuckles crack. Go for somewhere in the middle – a slightly firm and very confident handshake. "Ninety percent of what we think about a person is determined in the first ninety seconds we meet them." – Anonymous

Often times, this is offered in the almighty handshake.

At many of the events I attended, there seemed to be a cliquish environment. I cannot tell you how disappointing this made me feel knowing that I would either have to learn to be part of a clique or feel left out all. One thing that I have learned in my many years of networking is that most successful entrepreneurs never sit with the same people that they always sit with. Think about it. You already know these people, their business, and their network. They don't have the ability to offer you any new connections or information.

Obviously, this behavior will defeat their entire purpose of even being there. If you stick with the same circle of friends, then you're never going to meet anybody new, and the newcomers will look at your organization as a clique. This will just become a repetitive, non-productive behavior.

Some people will experience fear from going to a new group by themselves because they are afraid that no one will notice them. You will meet one every meeting. There are those who just come and quickly leave. They throw their business cards around the room, make loud noises and big hand gestures, but never make an effort to build a relationship. If you want to make a difference, stand out from the rest, and most importantly, remember you are there to build your business. Then, you need to be proactive. That means taking control of the situation and taking advantage of the opportunity instead of just reacting to it.

Becoming a successful networker means that you must go beyond your comfort zone and challenge yourself to do and be different. I've also attended many networking events and watched people who are unable to risk getting out of their comfort zone and saying hello to anybody. Some of these people are in sales, which is astonishing. I have also met some of the same people who, after a little bit of time and training, become the best networkers out there.

Your time is valuable, so let's get to work. Your goal is to find new people to network with, and believe it or not, it's their goal too. So, don't just sit around and warm up a chair or sit behind a table. Get up, connect, and get involved. If you happen to like the group, join it. Become a committee member, work on their board, or at least volunteer with some of the activities that they need help with.

One of my favorite strategies is to become a connector. Pretend that you're hosting the event. Greet people with a big smile and that nice firm handshake. Find out how to connect one person to the other. There are some great questions that you can ask that can help you facilitate this process.

The main point here, is to be actively friendly and approachable. People want to do business with people who are leaders. They'll be attracted and drawn toward those who want to help them. And don't forget, it's good karma. As you're helping others, before you know it, they'll be helping you.

A person who has achieved the skills of a great networker will be sincere as well as friendly. They will be a great listener and someone who can follow up and stay in touch. One of my favorite quotes is, "People will never remember what you say, they'll never remember what you've done, but they will always remember how you made them feel." Did you make your contacts feel like rock stars? Are they going to think of you first, when they are in the marketplace? How did you achieve that? Did you give them referrals and ideas without a thought to your own personal gain? Can people actually believe what you say is true? Did you do all of the talking or did you do a fair amount of listening?

What to Say:

In an open networking atmosphere, it operates just a little bit different than the strategic meetings. The strategic meeting, sometimes called lead groups, usually has a format they want you to follow. If you attend one of those types of meetings on a regular basis, then you definitely want to have at least six different ways within their format to express your referral request, usually within 30 seconds.

As mentioned before, these are called elevator speeches. Your referral request could be anything from an industry you're looking to partner with or a certain type of customer that you're looking for. Whatever it may be, the group is there to help you promote your content, so give them something to think about all day long, every-day of the week. Have them thinking of you every time they meet somebody that fits your ideal client. This is a huge opportunity for you to 'brand' yourself!

Also, make sure that your tagline, or the thought you leave them with, is something that is relevant to the group that you're visiting. Your company may do several things very well but when you're introducing yourself to somebody, you want to use the one thing that's going to really resonate with them. For example, if you're visiting a group that works with baby boomers and you happen to be a real estate agent, maybe your tagline could be, "I work with XYZ real estate company and we specialize in helping seniors downsize with less stress and more freedom."

For open networking, always remember this tip. He who asks the most questions wins. People love to share information about their world, knowledge, and experiences. What a great opportunity to listen and find a need that you can possibly help meet in the future. Begin your conversation with the basics such as your name, your company, your position, etc. Know your information well, and be able to recite it.

Who's First?

When it becomes open networking time, who do you talk to first? Do you have a strategy for this? When everybody else had their time to share, did you take notes? Who did you talk to and why? I always label my contact list with a 1 through 5 based on the priority of who I want to speak to first depending upon what I learned about them. Maybe they would be the perfect power partner, customer, or referral-base.

Ice breakers can be effective conversation starters:

How are you enjoying tonight?

Do you network often?

How about them Broncos? (Or whichever local sports team you guys support). What do you do for fun?

Bring up some vacation topics. This can give you an indication of what kind of lifestyle they live.

Do you help support nonprofits? Do you like to volunteer? This can give you an indication of where their heart is.

You can ask some qualifying questions:

What services or products does your company offer?

What does your best client or customer look like?

What makes you stand out from your competition?

A common problem that some business owners encounter is that they may not be the only person from their company or industry, and they want to know how to stand out. For one, don't stay in the same area. Circulate and keep involving yourself in different conversations. Don't be negative about your competition. Just take the chance to show how you stand out in your industry and what makes you shine.

People are going to want to do business with the ones they enjoy the most. Be that person. And understand, different personalities gravitate toward each other in different ways. Always remember, there are plenty of great customers to go around. If you understand and respect that, you'll have a lot more success.

There are different types of customers that you can be looking for while you're networking. These include customers that have needs, which they aren't aware of yet. Then there are people that have direct needs, and they let you know what those needs are. And then of course, there are some that have needs of which you can guess by listening very carefully, then you can align your offer to that specific need. At this point, you can direct a more targeted pitch.

Cultivate what you're asking for. Are you looking for referrals? New customers? Partnerships? Re-emphasize and always know your end goal. Active listening is very important, so don't be so focused on what you are trying to say that you fail to listen. When it's your time to talk, paraphrase part of their conversation back to them within your response. This helps to display that you were truly listening and that you can understand how they feel.

Watch their body language. Are they acting bored? Interested? This goes for the both of you, so pay attention to yours too. One thing to also remember is the term, power partners. These are the amazing people who work in and around the same type of clients and customers that you do but in a different industry. You can help share this database. For example, a great power partner for an electrician is a plumber, and a power partner for a real estate agent would be a mortgage broker. How about a bookkeeper and a banker? Or a photographer and a wedding planner? You get the idea?

The one thing to never forget to bring while networking is a thin black sharpie. Along my journey, I've learned that I always forget some of the finer details of all the wonderfully different people that I have met. So, as I'm talking to people, I always bring a little black Sharpie pen with me to make notes on the business cards, maybe denoting that they have two kids and a dog or maybe they were wearing a green jacket. This helps so much with memory recall later. It also helps me remember to appreciate every connection that I make.

Another really good tip is to bring your date book or planner so you can set coffee dates or other appointments right then. This is really a necessity, as it is why you are out networking in the first place.

The Most Common Networking Mistakes

- Always avoid potentially sensitive issues. Topics such as religion, politics or anything that could cause any discomfort in the conversation should be avoided.

- Don't tell classless jokes.

- Don't act bored when someone is speaking, look over their shoulder, or focus your eyes in other directions. Look them in the eye. Be present in the conversation.

- Turn your phone off or on silent. Your phone can be a distraction. If you happen to get a phone call, please excuse yourself and take it in private. Anything else makes you look impolite, rude, and arrogant.

- No interrupting. Just wait for them to finish even if what you have to say is really important. The only exception to that rule is if there's honestly a true emergency.

- Being overly loud and obnoxious is never a good way to be remembered.

- A lot of events serve alcohol, so it is very important to do all things in moderation.

- Walking up to group of people and just handing out your business card is definitely not a good idea. Talk about a pet peeve.

- Did I mention not to call someone else's baby ugly? This is not the time to bad- mouth any company. That includes your own. No trash-talking current employers or competitors. There is no way you're going to be given any value if in your neighborhood, the only way to make your house look bigger is to burn the everyone elses' house down. This is not a way to build relationships or any kind of respect in the business world.

- This is also not the time to bring up all your troubles and woes at home. The first person I disconnect to is the one I ask, "How is your day?" or "How is business?" and they start ranting about how everything sucks. I can promise you, that's the one person I don't need in my world at any time for any reason.

- Don't use unprofessional language.

- Don't leave early.

What about THAT person? You know, the one we described above. You can't seem to get away from them and they completely monopolize your time. Remember, you're on the clock, and this is your very valuable time to make contacts and meet your goals. You can excuse yourself and go to the restroom.

You can tell them, "Excuse me, I see someone I need to talk to." And that is the truth. You need at least five appointments from this event.

You can tell them that it was great meeting them, and you hope they have a wonderful time and meet lots of contacts as well. I personally like to introduce them to someone else I just met and say, "Oh my goodness, you have got to meet so and so," and then I politely excuse myself. Funny thing is that sometimes people just need to be connected to the right people. It's beautiful to watch relationships grow that you've actually had a hand in starting.

The Fortune Is In the Follow Up

Once the event is complete, don't forget to connect with all these people you just met, whether you need to connect with them on Facebook, Twitter, LinkedIn or other social media outlets. Log their email and their phone number and put everything in your follow-up system or your contact management system. Make notes and include different ways that you can help each other grow.

Remember networking is a two-way street. Don't expect new contacts to give you tons of referrals and business unless you are equally generous. You need to have a great follow-up system. How will you keep in touch with these new contacts? How will you share information or leads that might benefit them as well?

Trust me when I say, you'll be paid back tenfold for your thoughtfulness in helping others. The way I think about following up is that it is simply a second date with an opportunity to get to know more about them on a different level. Your goal is to see if they're good fit and a great referral source for you or not.

On a very important note, when someone sends you a referral and they will, we call this a hot lead or a golden ticket. Make sure you follow up very quickly with this lead because your contact put their reputation and friendship on the line for you, so make sure you honor that. Good rule of thumb is to contact them within 24 to 48 hours to set an appointment. Don't destroy the trust and the relationship by failing to take the referral seriously. Commit to organize your contacts so they don't become lost right after you make the connection. You need to find a good system that works for you and your business.

Note: It is never a good practice to sign people up for your newsletter or add them to your Facebook group without authorization. Never assume just because they met you and shook your hand that they want to be added into your world. Always get their express permission before you do these things. Many people become upset with this.

Treat your business like a job. You need to make sure you prioritize time for not only the networking event itself, but for the follow-up process, and the coffee dates as well.

Take It Up A Notch In Your Everyday Action Plan

Before I started taking networking seriously, I can remember when I first started my business and ran out of family and friends to connect with. I didn't know what to do next. Should I put an ad in the paper? A shout out on Facebook and get blocked from everybody I love? Then it hit me. As a representative of my company, I had to be what people thought of first when they found themselves in my community or in need of services from my industry.

I didn't know what to say or even how to say it. How do I create curiosity to get people to want to know more about me or my business? How do I get them to think of me first?

Now that I know the power of networking, I realized a neat trick. Whenever I was out in the community, on social media, or meeting different people in every day functions, I could utilize my relationship with my networking group to make conversation. I found great pleasure in adding value to others first before I asked them to add value to me.

By offering other people a way to grow their business, not only are you inviting them into your world, but you are facilitating changing theirs as well. You can also simply invite a contact you made out for a coffee date to get to know them better. Find out more about them and their goals are. What are their products or services? What kind of referrals are they looking for? How can you help them connect to others? In short, what value can you bring to them?

Never forget that wherever you are, you really are networking. Something as simple as a quick trip to the grocery store can be a networking opportunity. There are people everywhere you are. Are you networking everywhere you go? Are you listening to what's going on around you? Is there someone that may need your services or products? At your church, your gym, parties, school events, even on walks with your dog, always have your business cards with you.

One of my favorite games to play is the 3-foot rule game. As it seems, every three feet, there's a person, to be able to start a conversation with.

This is ultimately one of my favorite things to do. The Hunt. The fun challenge to myself. Some call this warm-chatting and some call it walk-n-talking. It's essentially meeting a stranger anywhere - the gas pump, down the aisle at the grocery store, in the dentist office – anywhere that there is a person within 3 feet of you. Create conversation. Create curiosity. Build a relationship. Ask for a follow up to further build a relationship upon a more solid foundation. Remember, every single person you meet knows at least 250+ people that you have yet to meet.

After talking to a lot of business owners, I found that many of them really don't know what to say outside of talking about who they are, their business, and what they're trying to sell.

What's wrong with saying, "Hey! I'm a member of this amazing networking group and I know there will be a lot of people who would love to hear about what you do. I too would like to get to know you and your business better, so I can know how to find the best referral for you. When's a good time to have coffee?"

Begin enjoying the art of meeting people. Learn to start conversations everywhere you go. Ask open-ended questions. Kick up your ability to listen for their needs and wants. Never forgetting, of course, odds are, at the same time they will ask you some of the same questions. Always, enter these appointments or coffee dates with the goal of building a true relationship so that you may guarantee a referral-based business for a lifetime. How many these appointments can you fit into your schedule this week? My goal is now fifteen. Start with one. Then increase to three until you reach fifteen as well.

When you purposely make networking a lifestyle and priority, you will experience unbelievable personal and business growth. Also, making positive connections will allow you to make a greater impact within your community and the customers you serve. Don't spend another penny on marketing without challenging yourself to make an intentional commitment to attending a networking event at least once a month. That is a good place to begin. As you become more accustomed to this lifestyle, increase your frequency to twice a month, then once a week. The results will speak for themselves, and you will become a networking master. Now, what are you waiting for? Get out your calendar, look up some events, and block out some dates, start building relationships, and make a difference in somebody's world today!